MARY PAGE MARLOWE

MARY PAGE MARLOWE

TRACY LETTS

THEATRE COMMUNICATIONS GROUP   NEW YORK   2016

Mary Page Marlowe is published by Theatre Communications Group, Inc., 520 Eighth Avenue, 24th Floor, New York, NY 10018-4156

The publication of *Mary Page Marlowe* by Tracy Letts, through TCG's Book Program, is made possible in part by the New York State Council on the Arts with the support of Governor Andrew Cuomo and the New York State Legislature.

TCG books are exclusively distributed to the book trade by Consortium Book Sales and Distribution.

Library of Congress Control Numbers:
2016039122 (print) / 2016045560 (ebook)
ISBN 978-1-55936-534-5 (paperback) / ISBN 978-1-55936-855-1 (ebook)
A catalog record for this book is available from the Library of Congress.

Book design and composition by Lisa Govan
Cover design by John Gall
Cover photo by Serge Giotti/Millennium Images

First Edition, December 2016
Second Printing, April 2020

FOR MOM

I think we are well advised to keep on nodding terms with the people we used to be, whether we find them attractive company or not. Otherwise they turn up unannounced and surprise us, come hammering on the mind's door at four A.M. of a bad night and demand to know who deserted them, who betrayed them, who is going to make amends.

—*Joan Didion*

MARY PAGE MARLOWE

PRODUCTION HISTORY

Mary Page Marlowe received its world premiere at Steppen-
wolf Theatre Company (Anna D. Shapiro, Artistic Director; David Schmitz, Managing Director) on April 10, 2016.
The production was directed by Anna D. Shapiro. The sce-
nic design was by Todd Rosenthal, the costume design was
by Linda Roethke, the lighting design was by Marcus Doshi,
the sound design was by Richard Woodbury, and the original
music was by Diana Lawrence; the production stage manager
was Malcolm Ewen. The cast was:

MARY PAGE MARLOWE

Ages 59, 63, 69	Blair Brown
Ages 27, 36	Carrie Coon
Age 50	Laura T. Fisher
Age 12	Caroline Heffernan
Age 19	Annie Munch
Ages 40, 44	Rebecca Spence
LOUIS GILBERT	Jack Edwards
WENDY GILBERT	Madeline Weinstein
LORNA	Tess Frazer
CONNIE	Ariana Venturi
ANDY	Alan Wilder
ED MARLOWE	Stephen Cefalu, Jr.
ROBERTA MARLOWE	Amanda Drinkall

SHRINK	Kirsten Fitzgerald
NURSE	Sandra Marquez
RAY	Ian Barford
DAN	Gary Wilmes
BEN	Keith D. Gallagher

CHARACTERS

MARY PAGE MARLOWE
Age 10 months
Age 12
Age 19
Ages 27, 36
Ages 40, 44
Age 50
Ages 59, 63, 69

LOUIS GILBERT

WENDY GILBERT

LORNA

CONNIE

ANDY

ED MARLOWE

ROBERTA MARLOWE

SHRINK

NURSE

RAY

DAN

BEN

NOTE

Wendy Gilbert, ages 16 and 20, should be played by the same actor. Roberta Marlowe, ages 19 and 32, should be played by the same actor.

SETTING

Various locations in Ohio and Kentucky.

SCENE 1

1986.

> *Mary Page Marlowe is forty.*
> *Her son, Louis, is twelve.*
> *Denny's. Dayton, Ohio.*

LOUIS: I get all these mixed up. *(Pause)* Can you keep these straight? I can't remember how they go. *(Pause)* Mom.

MARY PAGE: What.

LOUIS: Tell me how these go.

MARY PAGE: You don't know your states.

LOUIS: I always get these mixed up.

MARY PAGE: Do you have a geography class?

LOUIS: We had a unit.

MARY PAGE: What's that mean?

LOUIS: It was part of social studies.

MARY PAGE: They don't make you take geography? That should be the first thing you take. That should be Number One. Number Three. Reading, writing, geography.

LOUIS: Can you fill all these in?

MARY PAGE: Of course I can.

LOUIS: I get these four all mixed up.

MARY PAGE: You know this. 'Cause we've been there.

LOUIS: Nevada?

MARY PAGE: Have you been to Nevada?

LOUIS: I dunno.

MARY PAGE: You don't know.

LOUIS: Nope.

MARY PAGE: You don't know where you've been?

LOUIS: Nope.

MARY PAGE: What do you want for your birthday? You've got a birthday coming up.

LOUIS: Yeah.

MARY PAGE: Gonna be a teenager. God. *(Pause)* Do you know what you want?

LOUIS: M.A.S.K.

MARY PAGE: What's that? Like a disguise?

LOUIS: Mobile Armored Strike Kommand.

(Mary Page's daughter, Wendy, fifteen, enters, returning from the bathroom.)

MARY PAGE: You okay?

WENDY: I'm fine.

MARY PAGE: You didn't eat much.

WENDY: It's okay.

MARY PAGE: I know it's hard, honey. I'm sorry.

WENDY: Please stop looking at me.

MARY PAGE: I never wanted it to get like this. But you both have to know—Louis?—you both have to know that your father and I love you very much. This doesn't change the way we feel about you. This doesn't have anything to do with you. We tried everything we knew to make it work, and we worked for so long at it, 'cause we love you guys so much and we wanted you to have a house that was, you know, a loving house.

WENDY: So where do we go? Who's moving out?

MARY PAGE: Well, that's complicated. The house belongs to Sonny, to your father, you know it belonged to your grandma, so the house is his. And I got a job offer down in Lexington, a new job—

WENDY: So you're leaving.

MARY PAGE: Hold on, honey, it's complicated—

WENDY: Why can't you just say?

MARY PAGE: I am, I am saying. It's complicated, so just listen and let me explain it. I have to go down there and start my job. But we don't want to pull you guys out of school in the middle of a school year, so you'll stay here with your father and I'll come back and see you on the weekends. Then after—

WENDY: Where will you be on the weekends?

MARY PAGE: With you, here in Dayton, I'll be at the house with you. Your father will go to your Aunt Leigh's house.

WENDY: Just on the weekends.

MARY PAGE: Listen. Then sometime this summer you'll move down with me.

WENDY: Just for the summer.

MARY PAGE: No, to live with me. Permanently.

WENDY: In Kentucky?! Mom!

MARY PAGE: Wait, don't—

WENDY: Mom, I'm not living in fucking Kentucky!

MARY PAGE: Hey, watch your language, Wendy—

WENDY: Well, I'm not living in fucking Kentucky! I have two more years of high school! I'm not going to a new school my junior year! Not with all those fucking Kentucky hicks!

MARY PAGE: First of all, lower your voice—

WENDY: But it's not fucking fair!

MARY PAGE: —and second of all—

WENDY: Don't we get any say in what happens?!

MARY PAGE: —watch your—no, you don't get any say in what happens, because the adults are making the decisions—

WENDY: That's stupid, because the adults are making decisions about what they want, and we should get to say what *we* want!

MARY PAGE: You can say what you want, but that doesn't mean— you can say what you want. Let me hear what you want.

WENDY: I want to finish high school! Here!

MARY PAGE: Well, that's not possible, because I'm not going to be here. I'm going to be in Kentucky.

WENDY: Why don't you get a job here?

MARY PAGE: Because that's not the way it works. I looked for a job here but I couldn't find one. Where I found a job is in Lexington. We can all say what we want but we don't always get what we want. Louis, what do you want?

WENDY: Then I want to stay with Daddy, just while I'm in school, and then I'll come down and spend the summers with you.

MARY PAGE: That's not possible.

WENDY: Why?

MARY PAGE: Because that's not what your father wants.

WENDY: What does he want?

MARY PAGE: He wants something else.

WENDY: What?

MARY PAGE: He wants . . . he wants to keep you guys for the rest of the school year while I go down to Kentucky. He wants me to come up and stay with you on the weekends while he goes to stay at your Aunt Leigh's. He wants you to come down to Lexington to live with me starting this summer.

WENDY: So he gets exactly what he wants.

MARY PAGE: Yes.

WENDY: What do you want?

MARY PAGE: Your father and I talked about this and we agree about the way to do this. Wendy, please, I know this is hard—

WENDY: I wish you'd stop saying that.

MARY PAGE: I know this is hard, but it's the best solution to a bad problem.

WENDY: Why can't you just say what you want?

MARY PAGE: We'll get through this. We're just moving. We're just going to move.

WENDY: To Kentucky.

MARY PAGE: Do you really think Lexington is that much worse than Dayton?

WENDY: Yes!

MARY PAGE: Really?

WENDY: Mom, they're a bunch of hicks! They're coal miners!

MARY PAGE: What do you know about coal miners—?

WENDY: You know what I mean! I don't want to spend my last two years in high school with a bunch of hillbillies!

MARY PAGE: This isn't Paris. This isn't, y'know . . . *Tokyo*—

WENDY: No, Mom, God, don't make me finish high school in Kentucky.

MARY PAGE: Do you really think a couple of hundred miles makes that much difference? Every place is the same. And I have to say this, it's hard for you to see it now, this is sad, and it's not the way we wanted it, but this is not a tragedy. Two people . . . your dad and I fell out of love with each other, it's not like somebody died, or somebody got sick—

WENDY: Is that what happened, you and Daddy fell out of love?

MARY PAGE: Yes.

WENDY: That's what he says?

MARY PAGE: We agree that this is the way to do this.

WENDY: God, listen to you. It's like you're in the Kremlin.

MARY PAGE: Louis?

LOUIS: Yeah?

MARY PAGE: Do you have any questions, sweetie?

LOUIS: No.

MARY PAGE: Okay.

WENDY: What's your job?

MARY PAGE: The same job. Different firm.

WENDY: What happened to your old job?

MARY PAGE: I lost it.

WENDY: How'd you lose it?

MARY PAGE: They let me go.

WENDY: Why?

MARY PAGE: They no longer needed me.

WENDY: Why?

MARY PAGE: Wendy.

WENDY: Well, why?

LOUIS: What happens to Spooky?

MARY PAGE: Spooky will stay with you, in the house, in your dad's house. Then when you guys come live with me, Spooky will come with you. You can keep Spooky.

WENDY: Great. He can keep pissing on my choir robe down in Kentucky.

MARY PAGE: Maybe you'll hang up your choir robe in Kentucky.

WENDY: It's my fault the cat pisses on my stuff? *(Pause)* Like they even have choir in Kentucky.

MARY PAGE: Yes, they have choir in Kentucky. People don't stop singing just because they cross the state line.

WENDY: Daddy should be here for this conversation.

MARY PAGE: He thought I should be the one to tell you.

WENDY: He thought?

MARY PAGE: We thought.

WENDY: Are we still Gilberts?

MARY PAGE: What?

WENDY: Our name. Am I still Wendy Gilbert?

MARY PAGE: Yes. You're still Wendy Gilbert. You're still Louis Gilbert.

WENDY: Daddy's still Sonny Gilbert. What about you, are you still Mary Page Gilbert, or do you go back to your old name?

MARY PAGE: I haven't, I don't know. No, I'll go back to Marlowe.

WENDY: Who set that book on fire? *(Pause)* I came down for breakfast the other day and that book *Elephants Can Remember* was on the coffee table and a bunch of pages were burned in the back of it.

MARY PAGE: Dad and me . . . we've had some . . . we, uh . . . we've had a lot of . . . *(Pause)* This is really hard . . .

LOUIS: "Kentucky."

MARY PAGE *(Smiles, nods at Louis, long pause)*: Sometimes we do things we shouldn't do.

SCENE 2

1965.

> *Mary Page Marlowe is nineteen.*
> *Lorna and Connie are her college girlfriends.*
> *A dorm room. Dayton, Ohio.*

MARY PAGE: Let's keep going.

LORNA: Okay, Mary Page, this represents how you see your-self: good one, the Moon. Any time you get one of the Major Arcana, you've got to pay attention 'cause it has more impact. Connie, don't touch the cards.

MARY PAGE: It's more accurate? Than the others?

LORNA: No, just means pay attention.

CONNIE: Can I change the record?

LORNA: Kind of like it's underlined. It underlines it for you. So the moon, right, it's all about rhythm and nature, the rhythm of nature—

MARY PAGE: —uh-huh—

LORNA: —and how that's part of us, it's elemental. 'Cause it affects the tides and your time of the month and everything, so it's kind of about your ESP.

CONNIE: Oooh, like mind control?

LORNA: More like just your intuition. I mean, the way you know your way around in your room even when the lights are off? With the moon, it's dark, but because of your ESP, you can see anyway. The moon means you see it all by moonlight, right?

CONNIE: What the hell. That's how she sees herself?

MARY PAGE: I don't get it.

CONNIE: I love this song—

LORNA: No, but remember, it's in context of the question you asked yourself before the reading.

CONNIE: What was the question you asked yourself?

LORNA: She can't say.

CONNIE: That's so stupid. When you make a wish, you can't say or it won't come true. Guess what, it's not coming true anyway, so you might as well say it out loud and stop boring us all to death.

MARY PAGE: Wait, Lorna, just tell me what the Moon card means here.

LORNA: "Things are not what they appear to be."

MARY PAGE: Okay. That makes sense.

LORNA: So that speaks to your question.

MARY PAGE: Yes, 'cause . . . nope, got it.

CONNIE: C'mon, like we don't know your question isn't about Robert Bedwell.

LORNA: She can't say!

CONNIE: You read my cards after and I'll tell you exactly what my question is and it's about *boys*, I can tell you that much.

MARY PAGE: My question is not about Robert. It's about *me*. And Robert. Come on, Lorna, what's next?

LORNA: Okay, so this card is about how others see you.

CONNIE: There's a Big Slut card?

LORNA: Connie, stop it, you need to pay attention.

CONNIE: All right.

LORNA: It makes a difference to the reading.

CONNIE: The cards are already dealt. You already dealt the cards.

LORNA: But your energy affects the cards!

CONNIE: They're already dealt! Nothing we do is gonna change the cards!

MARY PAGE: Come on, we're almost done, then we can do you.

CONNIE: Goodie.

LORNA: How others see you: ooooh, the Queen of Cups.

CONNIE: Queen of the B-Cup.

LORNA: Connie—

MARY PAGE: Come on.

LORNA: Queen of Cups is a great card for you, I can't believe you got it, 'cause if I had to pick one card out of the deck that says how I see you, this would be it. The Queen of Cups. This is all about hope, and dreams, and possibilities. Everything is possible with the Queen of Cups, it's like she's falling in love, and sometimes she can indicate pregnancy. With this card, you just dream, whatever it is that you dream about, she is really just letting yourself do that.

MARY PAGE: That's how you see me.

LORNA: Yes.

CONNIE: That's how I see you.

MARY PAGE: No, you don't.

CONNIE: Yeah. I do.

MARY PAGE: As all that. All that . . . hope and love and dreams.

CONNIE: Yeah.

LORNA: Like that day you read that sonnet in Dr. Lundergan's class. And everybody was just silent. You cast this spell, like you had this light around your head, like a halo. Like you glowed.

CONNIE: I don't know if you *glowed*, but yeah, I think of you like that.

MARY PAGE: I don't know what to say. You guys are embarrassing me.

CONNIE: We love you. You think we'd be best friends with someone we don't love?

MARY PAGE: What's the next card?

LORNA: Your greatest hope . . . and your greatest fear.

CONNIE: *That* doesn't make any sense.

LORNA: Sure it does. What's your greatest hope?

CONNIE: That I'm a millionaire.

LORNA: And what's your greatest fear?

CONNIE: Korean soldiers stabbing me to death in a deep freezer.

(Pause.)

LORNA *(To Mary Page)*: Okay. Your greatest hope . . . and your greatest fear. *(Turns card)* Two of Wands. I have to look at the book.

CONNIE: You lose all credibility when you look in that book.

MARY PAGE: She's learning.

LORNA: I want to get it right.

CONNIE: Yeah, 'cause that would be a drag, if you got the *future wrong*. *(To Mary Page)* What happened with you and Robert Bedwell last night?

MARY PAGE: Robert. He's Robert. Why do you say his full name like that?

CONNIE: Give me a break, his last name is *Bedwell*.

MARY PAGE: What makes you think anything happened?

CONNIE: You've been acting like a weirdo.

MARY PAGE: He proposed.

CONNIE: What?!

LORNA: He what?!

CONNIE: He proposed.

MARY PAGE: He did.

CONNIE: Where? What did he do? Did he get down on one knee? What did he say? Did he have a ring?

MARY PAGE: I don't have a ring.

CONNIE: Why not? Where's the ring? Mary Page, where is your ring?!

MARY PAGE: I said no.

CONNIE: You did what?

MARY PAGE: I said no. I turned him down, flat. I don't want to marry Robert, and I don't want to get married right now.

LORNA: You're so great.

MARY PAGE: I've gotten to know him better, and . . . I don't think that's what I want for my life.

LORNA: Good for you—

CONNIE: He's gorgeous! He's the most handsome boy on campus!

MARY PAGE: I know. But he's . . . he's very immature.

CONNIE: He's Catholic.

MARY PAGE: I don't care.

LORNA: He drinks too much.

MARY PAGE: Look in your book, Lorna.

LORNA: Okay.

MARY PAGE: It's not just him. I don't know. I don't want to be married. I just feel too independent for all that, or . . . I just don't want to be married. I'm interested in other things. It's not like that's my only choice in life. Are you going to marry Al?

CONNIE: That's different, Al's half Greek. I can't marry a Greek.

MARY PAGE: Why not? He's Catholic.

CONNIE: No, that's a whole different kind of Catholic, very hairy, a lot more incense.

MARY PAGE: Then don't give me a hard time.

CONNIE: Then what do you want to do instead?

MARY PAGE: I don't know. Travel? Get out of Ohio, I hate it here. Wouldn't you like to see what else is out there?

CONNIE: We don't have any rich uncles. We would need *jobs*.

MARY PAGE: I want to see Paris.

CONNIE: You've been hung up on Paris ever since we saw *Charade*. You want to be Audrey Hepburn.

MARY PAGE: What's wrong with that?

CONNIE: It's a *movie*. She's *Audrey Hepburn*.

MARY PAGE: So? I'll be me.

LORNA: Which brings us back to the Two of Wands. It's really about destiny. So it's appropriate that it comes up as your hope-and-fear card. 'Cause what it's saying is that you are in charge of your own destiny. It's up to you to decide what you want to do. And see how that could be your greatest hope and your greatest fear? Nothing is going to let you off the hook. You're responsible.

CONNIE: There you go. You want out of here so bad? You have to do it yourself.

MARY PAGE: Okay, so the last card is . . . ?

LORNA: The outcome.

MARY PAGE: Lorna, wait. I'm nervous. Isn't that weird?

LORNA: I don't think it's weird.

MARY PAGE: What if it's the Death card?

LORNA: The Death card isn't bad.

CONNIE: Of course the Death card is bad.

LORNA: It's not.

CONNIE: It's the *Death* card.

LORNA: It's just about transitions.

CONNIE *(To Mary Page)*: The Death card is bad. But you shouldn't be scared.

MARY PAGE: Why not?

CONNIE: Because the card has already been dealt.

SCENE 3

2009.

   Mary Page Marlowe is sixty-three.
   Her husband, Andy, is around the same age.
   Their home. Versailles, Kentucky.

MARY PAGE: Andy, it's starting!
ANDY *(From off)*: Well, pause it!
MARY PAGE: I don't know how.
ANDY *(From off)*: Hit the pause button.
MARY PAGE: How can you pause it?
ANDY *(From off)*: Oh my God . . .
MARY PAGE: I still don't get it.

   (Andy enters with food, pauses the TV.)

ANDY: You can pause it now.
MARY PAGE: But isn't it live? It's not recorded.

ANDY: When you paused it, you started recording.

MARY PAGE: But isn't it playing? Somewhere, live?

ANDY: Yes, which is why you can rewind it, because you're recording it.

MARY PAGE: Can you fast-forward it?

ANDY: Yes.

MARY PAGE: That does not compute. 'Cause that would mean you could fast-forward the news, and then we would know the future.

ANDY: You can only fast-forward up to the point when it's live.

MARY PAGE: The whole thing is live! The whole thing is happening, right now!

ANDY (*Laughing*): You're recording it!

MARY PAGE: I don't get it!

ANDY: Goddamn it, Mary Page, we are going to solve this, once and for all.

MARY PAGE: I'm hungry.

ANDY: Let's eat. I'm going to explain this to you.

MARY PAGE: That smells fantastic.

ANDY: Okay, so they are broadcasting *House, M.D.* tonight on the FOX television network.

MARY PAGE: Don't patronize me.

ANDY: I'm just putting the ball on the tee. The show begins at eight P.M., and runs for an hour. At 8:10, you hit the pause button—

MARY PAGE: It's only 8:04.

ANDY: This is just by way of illustration.

MARY PAGE: No, say what's actually happening. Mm, I'm hungry.

ANDY: Here, eat. Don't forget the parmesan.

MARY PAGE: Okay. Is this the fancy stuff?

ANDY: It's parmesan. All right. At 8:10 you hit the pause button.

MARY PAGE: Let's just watch the show.

ANDY: You're an intelligent person. I want you to understand this. So at 8:10 you hit the pause button.

MARY PAGE: You forgot the part where at 8:05 you say, "You know he's an Englishman."

ANDY: I did not forget it, it's just not important. So at 8:10 you hit the pause button—

MARY PAGE: If it's not important, why do you always say it—?

ANDY: So at 8:10, you hit the pause button—

MARY PAGE: You know I've stopped listening.

ANDY: At 8:10, you hit the pause button!

MARY PAGE: I've moved on.

ANDY: Eat your spaghetti. Goddamn it, you are so goddamned stubborn—

MARY PAGE: Oh Lord . . .

ANDY: What? No good?

MARY PAGE: Garlic . . .

ANDY: Is there too much garlic? *(Laughing)* If you can't talk, that may mean there's too much garlic.

MARY PAGE: It's good . . .

ANDY: Yeah, I can tell by your gasping.

MARY PAGE: It really is good, it's just going to be hard to keep my friends.

(He laughs, recovers, laughs again.)

ANDY: You don't have any friends.

(They laugh.)

MARY PAGE: I have you. You're a pretty good friend.

ANDY: I'm not your friend, I'm your husband.

MARY PAGE: You're a pretty good husband, too.

(They kiss.)

ANDY: Are we watching?

(She nods. They watch while they eat.)

You know he's an Englishman.
MARY PAGE: Yeah . . .

(They watch.)

ANDY: He reminds me a lot of my first wife.
MARY PAGE: You mean the sarcastic know-it-all part.
ANDY: Uh-huh.
MARY PAGE: Not the brilliant surgeon part.
ANDY: No. And not the limpy drug-addict part.
MARY PAGE: Right.
ANDY: House is not a surgeon.
MARY PAGE: He performs surgery.
ANDY: He's a diagnostician.
MARY PAGE: He performs surgery.
ANDY: Yes.
MARY PAGE: The defense rests.

(They eat. They watch.)

You know why people like this show?
ANDY: Hm.
MARY PAGE: It lets them believe in resurrection.

(Andy pauses the DVR, produces an envelope, hands it to Mary Page.)

What's this?
ANDY: Open it.
MARY PAGE: Is this mine?
ANDY: Yes. Open it.
MARY PAGE: Did you open my mail?

ANDY: I did.

MARY PAGE: You read my mail?

ANDY: I did.

MARY PAGE: And then you saved it until *House* was on?

ANDY: You are correct. Again.

MARY PAGE: Oh my.

ANDY: Congratulations.

MARY PAGE: Why didn't you . . . ? Oh my.

ANDY: "Free at last."

(She weeps.)

Oh honey . . .

(He hugs her.)

MARY PAGE: I don't know why I'm crying.

ANDY: Well, it's a big deal.

MARY PAGE: It is a big deal.

ANDY: It's been a part of your life for a long time now.

MARY PAGE: A long time.

ANDY: You know what this means.

MARY PAGE: It means . . . it means a lot.

ANDY: It does.

MARY PAGE: It means I can leave the state . . .

ANDY: That's right, and we can go see Wendy and the kids.

MARY PAGE: Yeah, and leave when we want to . . .

ANDY: We can take our vacation, to San Francisco.

MARY PAGE: We can go anywhere we want.

ANDY: That's right, we can go anywhere we want.

MARY PAGE: It means I don't have to pee in a cup anymore.

ANDY: It means you don't have to see Julie anymore.

MARY PAGE: Oh, Julie. I should call her.

ANDY: Really? Why?

MARY PAGE: Just to say . . . well, I don't know.

ANDY: How about just to say, "Fuck you, Julie, I don't need your permission for anything anymore."

MARY PAGE: She's just doing her job.

ANDY: You've always been more forgiving of her than—

MARY PAGE: She's just doing her job, she doesn't have any stake in it. I know the women she has to deal with and her job is no picnic, believe me. I wouldn't do it.

(Pause.)

It's not the kind of good news you call people with though, is it? Not that I have a lot to call.

ANDY: You want to call Wendy?

MARY PAGE: No.

ANDY: Well, it's good news you can share with me.

MARY PAGE: Yeah . . .

ANDY: Jailbird. I guess I'll have to stop calling you that . . .

(Mary Page weeps. Andy holds her.)

Shhh. It's okay. It's okay. It's over.

SCENE 4

1946.

   Mary Page Marlowe is ten months old.
   She is in a crib.
   Her parents' house, living room. Dayton, Ohio.
   Voices come from off: a muffled, indistinct argument.
   Ed Marlowe, twenties, enters, crosses to a wet bar, gets a glass,
pours whiskey.
   Indistinct voice from off.

ED *(Offhand, calling into another room)*: I don't give a good goddamn.

   (Indistinct voice from off. Ed sits, drinks.)

   (To himself, mainly) I can't hear you.

   (Roberta, nineteen, enters.)

ROBERTA: I don't care how often you see your buddies, or when you see them. You can move in with them for all I care.

ED: We're gonna sit here and drink beers. And it's not just my buddies, he's bringing the Randall sisters with him.

ROBERTA: Who in hell are the Randall sisters?

ED: You know 'em.

ROBERTA: I don't know them.

ED: Louanne's the older one, works out at Streak's.

ROBERTA: That fat bucktooth whore is coming into my house?

ED: She ain't fat.

ROBERTA: You got women coming into our house now? While we got a baby sitting here?

ED: It's just a get-together.

ROBERTA: Is that what they're calling it now?

ED: If you don't like it, take the baby with you and go.

ROBERTA: You think I'm going to leave my house with our baby so you can get drunk with some roadhouse heifer?

ED: And her sister.

ROBERTA: You rotten son-of-a-bitch.

ED: I didn't say you had to leave. If you want, put Mary in our bed, and you stay in here and drink with us. All I said was they were coming is all.

ROBERTA: Arch came last night.

ED: He's coming tonight too.

ROBERTA: You said we were going to have an evening together, just us.

ED: I said we'd have dinner.

ROBERTA: You said a quiet evening.

(He does not respond.)

You said a quiet evening!

(He does not respond. She exits. He pours another whiskey. She reenters, wearing a coat.)

Just sit down with me, have a meal. Just lay down with me, let's talk. Let's get Mom to watch Mary Page and you and me can go out. Ed. I like to have a good time, I like to go out, I like to dance, I like to drink with our friends. All I want is for you to talk to me.

ED: I talk to you.

ROBERTA: You don't. Ever since . . . you don't, you won't talk. Tell me.

ED: Tell you what.

ROBERTA: Tell me what happened over there so terrible you don't want to talk to me anymore.

ED: Nothing happened.

ROBERTA: I'm going to Mom's.

ED: Take Mary with you.

ROBERTA: Nah. You can look after her tonight.

ED: Roberta—

ROBERTA: What? She's your kid too. You look after her. Maybe Louanne can help. Me, I'm going out.

ED: Roberta, I'm—

ROBERTA: Screw you!

(Roberta exits. Ed crosses to the crib, looks in. Crosses to the bar, finishes his drink.

He returns to the crib, sings softly to Mary Page:)

ED:

Saloon, saloon, saloon.
Runs through my brain like a tune.
You can keep your cafés, and I hate cabarets,
But just mention saloon and my cares fade away.

(He lifts Mary Page out of the crib, continues singing to her:)

For it brings back a fond recollection
Of a little old low-ceiling room
With a bar and a rail and a dime and a pail,
Saloon, saloon, saloon.

Since you've left us the world seems in darkness,
Like a cloud passing over the moon,
No more joys in my life, no more lies to my wife,
Saloon, saloon, saloon.

SCENE 5

1982.

> *Mary Page Marlowe is thirty-six.*
> *Her shrink is older.*
> *The shrink's office. Dayton, Ohio.*

SHRINK: You've never mentioned that before.

MARY PAGE: I don't think about it. Every now and again, just a fleeting . . . "Oh, right, I did that." Do the math, figure out the birthday. But I don't have any regrets about it. It more or less ended my relationship with the church 'cause I just couldn't . . . not that my relationship with the church was really profound but . . .

SHRINK: What I find interesting is that we've been seeing each other for a while and you've never . . . not even in passing have you—

MARY PAGE: Because it's not relevant, that's what I'm telling you, it feels like a different person who was going through that.

SHRINK: It was a big deal at the time, wasn't it?

MARY PAGE: Sure, at the time.

SHRINK: You were conflicted.

MARY PAGE: Yes.

SHRINK: And we've discussed a lot of things in here that you might not consider significant, but we—

MARY PAGE: This isn't a betrayal. I haven't kept something from you, intentionally. If I were keeping something from you, believe me, I wouldn't mention it now.

SHRINK: Do you have other things you're not mentioning?

MARY PAGE: I'm still a person outside of this room, you know. I still live life even when you're not watching me.

SHRINK: You seem defensive.

MARY PAGE: Because you seem upset!

SHRINK: I'm not upset.

MARY PAGE: Your tone is very accusing.

SHRINK: I want to know why you feel like you need to protect me from certain information.

MARY PAGE: It's a minor detail.

SHRINK: I don't consider it minor. Decisions like those, though it may not affect you today, in your day-to-day, they can impact other decisions you've made in your life. Does Sonny know? Was it his?

MARY PAGE: No, it was before I met Sonny, it was college.

SHRINK: Does he know?

MARY PAGE: He's Catholic.

SHRINK: What does that have to do with it?

MARY PAGE: No, he doesn't know.

SHRINK: But what does that have to do with it, that he's Catholic?

MARY PAGE: He's devout. Not devout, he's a believer. He believes that stuff, he would think that I'm going to hell. I don't know, maybe not literally. He would have an opinion about it.

SHRINK: So what if he has an opinion about it? Isn't that a conversation you get to have?

MARY PAGE: *Get* to have, no, I don't *want* to have that conversation.

SHRINK: Why, because you think he's right?

MARY PAGE: He has his beliefs and I have mine.

SHRINK: And you can't talk about the difference in your beliefs?

MARY PAGE: I don't *want* to.

SHRINK: Why not?

MARY PAGE: There's a lot we don't talk about. By agreement.

SHRINK: You've both agreed to that?

MARY PAGE: Yes.

SHRINK: Stated agreement.

MARY PAGE: Tacit agreement.

SHRINK: Tacit agreement. So he doesn't necessarily know what he's agreed to.

MARY PAGE: There are things we don't like about each other but it's not a good idea to pick at all that. We both work full time, we're exhausted, the freaking kids drive us up the wall. Louis is a disaster, he's eight years old and still wetting the bed. Sonny and I don't have the energy to sit around and talk about our feelings.

SHRINK: So you and Sonny don't discuss the difference in your beliefs, you don't talk about your feelings, as long as you're both separate but equal, everything's fine.

MARY PAGE: Yes. Yes.

SHRINK: Except everything is not fine, is it? I mean, there's a reason you seek out these extramarital affairs. And you don't like them, they don't make you feel better. According to you.

MARY PAGE: My life with Sonny is a life, it's a part of my life, but it isn't my whole life, I have a different life aside from my family, and we've discussed this, you and I have talked about compartments, and ways in which I might integrate the different lives. Oh, I'm exhausted, this . . .

SHRINK: No, now you're getting at something, finish that thought.

MARY PAGE: I can't. "Compartments." "Integrate." Now I talk like you. What bullshit words. What a nothing problem. I just found out my college girlfriend Lorna died from breast cancer last month and I'm sitting here talking about compartments. The truth is you and I pretend I make decisions about the direction of my life. I don't. I haven't. I didn't decide on any of it. All of it happened *to* me, and I went along with it, and I, I . . . I never affected anything, I never altered the course. Like some bird. Like a migrating bird. I just did what seemed natural.

SHRINK: And something about that feels wrong to you?

MARY PAGE: No. *(Not challenging)* Did I say wrong?

SHRINK: Seems like it bothers you.

MARY PAGE: Eh. Maybe. *(Laughs, thinks)* Just seems like, why did I bother, you know?

SHRINK: Bother with what?

MARY PAGE: Why would you ever get upset about anything, any decision, any dilemma, any job, any relationship, any anything, why lose sleep over it if it's all just accidental? Someone else could have written my diary.

SHRINK: You feel that unexceptional.

MARY PAGE: I *am* unexceptional.

SHRINK: You know, Mary Page, I hear you say this, about feeling—

MARY PAGE: Mm, it's just Mary now. No Page.

SHRINK: This is new.

MARY PAGE: Mm-hm.

SHRINK: Why did you do that?

MARY PAGE: I don't know.

SHRINK: You don't?

(Mary Page shakes her head.)

Well, I find that interesting.

MARY PAGE: Really? Not everything means something. I just got tired of it, explaining it. Spelling it.

SHRINK: But here, don't you see, you just finished telling me you didn't feel as if you had agency in your own life, and yet you changed your name.

MARY PAGE: I didn't change it.

SHRINK: Well . . . yes, you did.

MARY PAGE: I . . . okay, I . . . okay, yes.

SHRINK: You don't find that significant.

MARY PAGE: I don't. I do not. *(Pause)* And if I did . . . if it was significant . . . it's not very significant. When I talk about not making choices in my life, I'm not talking about . . . appearances.

SHRINK: So what are you talking about?

MARY PAGE *(Exasperated)*: Really? You don't know?

SHRINK: You tell me.

MARY PAGE: Ughh . . . I, I don't, this is the stuff that just feels like navel-gazing to me, and I—

SHRINK: Well, here we are, you're here, let's . . . gaze at it.

MARY PAGE: Okay. Sorry, what's the exercise?

SHRINK: You've said that you don't feel you've made choices in your life. And I want to know what would your life look like if you could make all the choices. Make them, remake them. Tell me, if you're calling the shots, calling all the shots.

MARY PAGE: Okay.

(Long pause. Thirty seconds, actually.)

I didn't do a good job of saying what I meant originally. Anything I say now is going to sound small, and immature. Because if I say, oh I'd live in Paris, I seem shallow, like my surroundings are the cause of my problems, or like I'm grousing about the lack of opportunities when I know in reality I've had a lot of opportunities. I just think that as a woman, a lot of our roles get stipulated for us, and there's only one way to be a wife, be a daughter, be a mom. Be a lover. Even my affairs, you know, you'd think that might be the one area of my life where I could break out and just be the person I am without the play-acting, because you don't have anything invested in the affair, there's no future or potential, so why not just drop it and be who you really are, but even there, I'm acting out a part, this easy girl, kind of dirty, won't make trouble. And it's horseshit, it's just playing a part for whoever the guy is, acting for him like the reason I'm doing this has something to do with sex. Sex with him, specifically, like he has anything to do with it. I mean the sex is fine, all of it works, and maybe I even get turned on by breaking the rules, but none of that is why I'm there. I've never once, not once in my life, had sex because of lust. The only rea-son I've ever had sex is shame, guilt, power, attention. No one will ever know that. No one is ever going to *see* me. Sonny and the kids are never going to *see* me. I'm not the person I am. I'm just *acting* like a person who is a wife and a mother. I know what that means, I know the levers to pull to be that person. I'm a great actress.

SHRINK: You're not the person you are.

MARY PAGE: No.

SHRINK: Then who are you?

MARY PAGE: I don't know.

SHRINK *(Quietly)*: What I'm asking you is, who is the person pulling the levers?

MARY PAGE: I don't know.

SCENE 6

2015.

> *Mary Page Marlowe is sixty-nine.*
> *The Nurse (Mary) is younger.*
> *A hospital room. Lexington, Kentucky.*
> *Mary Page has a thermometer in her mouth.*

NURSE: You eat lunch yet?

(Mary Page rolls her eyes. Beep. Nurse removes the thermometer.)

MARY PAGE: Do I still have one?

NURSE: You want lunch?

MARY PAGE: Do I still have a temperature?

NURSE: Yeah, just the same.

MARY PAGE: I ate lunch. It was awful.

NURSE: Did you eat it? What did you have?

MARY PAGE: Yes, I ate it. Turkey and gravy. The gravy was glowing yellow. It looked like something from *The Nutty Professor*.

NURSE: Did you want something else?

MARY PAGE: No. Are you new?

NURSE: No, I normally do weekend nights here.

MARY PAGE: What's your name?

NURSE: Mary.

MARY PAGE: Hi, Mary.

NURSE: Hi.

MARY PAGE: I'm Mary Page.

NURSE: I know. Where's the Page come from?

MARY PAGE: Family.

NURSE: Was that your daughter in here?

MARY PAGE: How could you tell?

NURSE: She looks just like you.

MARY PAGE: You got kids?

NURSE: Mm-hm. Five.

MARY PAGE: You do not have five kids.

NURSE: I do.

MARY PAGE: Can you remember all their names?

NURSE: Yeah.

MARY PAGE: You look too young to have five kids.

NURSE: Not really.

MARY PAGE: Well . . . I'm happy for you. Five children, that's a bounty.

NURSE: Big family. My grandmother has two hundred great-grandchildren.

MARY PAGE: Wow. She was fruitful, and multiplied.

NURSE: Yeah. She's still in Guatemala. But we're all going down there next year.

MARY PAGE: Wow.

NURSE: You got other kids or is your daughter your only one?

MARY PAGE: Just one, just Wendy. She has two kids. Small family. My husband said, "We're like the Kennedys but without the children or the power or the money."

NURSE: What does your husband do?

MARY PAGE: He's dead.

NURSE: Oh.

MARY PAGE: So he doesn't do much.

NURSE: I'm sorry.

MARY PAGE: He died a few years ago. Four years ago.

NURSE: I'm sorry.

MARY PAGE: I miss him. We weren't married that long, just a few years. He was my third husband. I wish I could have found him sooner, but . . . doesn't work that way.

NURSE: Three husbands.

MARY PAGE: Yeah.

NURSE: Can you remember all their names?

(Mary Page laughs heartily.)

MARY PAGE: Andy. He was the best one. *(Pause)* I'm dying. *(Pause)* It's okay. I know it. You can say it. It's okay. I'm ready.

NURSE: That's good.

MARY PAGE: I've had a *good* life. I've done a lot of the things I wanted to do. There were some places I wish I could have visited, but. I still got to go some places, see some things. I liked my work.

NURSE: What did you do?

MARY PAGE: I was a CPA.

NURSE: Oh. You liked it?

MARY PAGE: Yeah, I liked it. I never made a lot of money, and the politics in the office could get pretty . . . I struggled with a lot of that. But I liked doing taxes.

NURSE: Really? That seems like the boring part.

MARY PAGE: No, that's the interesting part of the job. Client comes in, drops a shoebox full of paperwork on the desk, "I made this much," feds withheld this much, and all of it seems pretty impersonal, but then you start to get into that shoebox and pick apart that paperwork—this receipt was for this dinner, this charge was for this birthday present, this was for flowers, this was for travel—like working a puzzle and putting the pieces in place—and sometimes it all comes together. All the numbers add up.

NURSE: Do the numbers always add up?

MARY PAGE: No. The numbers do not always add up. *(Pause)* I wasn't a *great* mom. But I liked it. I liked being a mom.

NURSE: So . . . no regrets, that's good.

MARY PAGE: I didn't say that. Couple of doozies. But who doesn't? Who wouldn't do some things different if they could?

NURSE: Right.

MARY PAGE: It takes such a long time to figure some things out.

NURSE: What did you figure out?

(Mary Page smiles, looks away, shakes her head. The Nurse hands her a box of tissues.)

MARY PAGE: Thank you, Mary. *(Pause)* What are your kids' names?

NURSE: Felipe, Marina, Sofia, Alfonso, and Ernie.

MARY PAGE: Good names. Ernie.

NURSE: Yeah . . .

MARY PAGE: I like it.

SCENE 7

1996.

Mary Page Marlowe is fifty.
Her face is bruised. She wears a soft cast on her wrist.
Her husband, Ray, is around her age.
Their home. Lexington, Kentucky.

MARY PAGE: She says Mr. Lopresto is going to live though he's in pretty bad shape, still in the hospital. He doesn't have any close family members raising hell with the DA's office. Angry family members, especially if they have money, can be influential in things like this. She said that. But Mr. Lopresto is single, he's a widower, no children, and if he has any close family, no one's come forward. Um, two things are considered "aggravating factors": my third DUI within five years, and the fact that I blew a point-three-two.

RAY: Jesus—

MARY PAGE: But she said the DA doesn't want to go to trial, for a lot of reasons but mainly because I'm a fifty-year-old woman, and so they're willing to plead me out.

RAY: And so what does that mean for sentencing?

MARY PAGE: The judge still has a lot of discretion. The lawyer says . . . "sentencing guidelines in terms of length of incarceration." Mmm, "only have to serve twenty percent before eligible for parole." *Eligible*. No guarantees there.

RAY: But what are those sentencing guidelines?

MARY PAGE: Five to ten years.

RAY: Oh my God. Mary Page.

MARY PAGE: But the judge apparently still has some leeway. The lawyer thinks I could get ten years, but then if you consider the twenty percent, I may only serve two years. She kept saying "one or two years actual time served," but she doesn't know, she can't make those guarantees.

RAY: I'm, I'm sorry, I don't know anything about this—

MARY PAGE: Let me finish. Mm, "judge's discretion . . . fines, community service." Restitution for the victim, I guess the court can order that I pay a certain amount of restitution. How that would impact any kind of civil suit brought by Mr. Lopresto she couldn't say. We'll cross that bridge when we come to it. And I'll lose my driving privileges for . . . well, for a long time. Maybe for life, who knows. That's it.

RAY: What if we fight this?

MARY PAGE: There's nothing to fight. There is no case that I am going to win in court.

RAY: You could plead not guilty.

MARY PAGE: I would be found guilty. That is a guarantee.

RAY: Why a guarantee?

MARY PAGE: Because I'm guilty.

RAY: A lot of guilty people don't go to prison.

MARY PAGE: I would be found guilty. They would find me guilty.

RAY: What about the patrolman? Wasn't he supposed to say what the charge was when he arrested you?

MARY PAGE: He makes the arrest and gathers the information but the charge is determined later.

RAY: Did he read you your rights?

MARY PAGE: You've asked me that three times now. Yes. He did.

RAY: He was very rough with you. Isn't there some option where we could get it thrown out if we could show he had been—?

MARY PAGE: We'd never be able to prove anything like that.

RAY: Why not? You were bruised, you had those bruises on your—

MARY PAGE: I'm still bruised, my whole body is one massive—

RAY: I'm talking about your wrists, you had those bruises on your wrists from where he—

MARY PAGE: I blew a point-three-two. I can't get on the stand and challenge the word of the cop. That point-three-two is going to be like a neon sign over my head. I'm sorry, Ray, I am going to do time.

RAY: Is there some sort of facility where you'd be housed with women who are nonviolent, that sort of thing?

MARY PAGE: There is no country club option. I'll most likely go to the state penitentiary at . . . Pee Wee? She kept saying Pee Wee.

RAY: Pewee Valley, it's outside Louisville.

MARY PAGE: I'll be in the general population. She also said I might serve some or even all of my time at County. She said they often put nonviolent offenders in County but that I'd actually prefer the penitentiary.

RAY: Why is that?

MARY PAGE: Um, they have programs, work programs, recreation. Counseling. County is just a lockup and a year or two is a long time to spend in lockup. It's twenty-three hours a day locked up.

RAY: How soon do we have to make a decision?

MARY PAGE: What decision? There's no decision. I told her to call the DA's office and get the ball rolling.

RAY: Why did you do that?

MARY PAGE: I didn't see the point in waiting.

RAY: The point in waiting is so we could talk about it first.

MARY PAGE: Ray, I'm telling you everything she said, but there's no decision to be made here. I am going to do this time.

(Pause.)

RAY: Goddamn it, I told you to get some help! Didn't I?! I told you that your drinking was out of control! You're killing yourself!

MARY PAGE: Is this why we need to take some time? So you can yell at me?

RAY: Yes! So I could get a chance to . . . fucking deal with this! My wife is going to prison, and I . . . I don't get a say in it!

MARY PAGE: No. You don't.

RAY: The night of our wedding, for God's sake, when you got so goddamn hammered, you passed out at your own goddamn reception!

MARY PAGE: Is this really the time for us to have that argument?

RAY: I was humiliated! Forget everybody else who saw it happen, my *mother* watched me and Wendy picking you up and carrying you out to the car!

MARY PAGE: I think I've apologized for that—

RAY: I'm not asking for an apology! I'm saying it was an indication that maybe something is wrong and that you need help!

MARY PAGE: Well, I'm paying the price for it now, aren't I?

RAY: I don't want you to pay a price, I want you to get better! You're my wife, Mary Page, I love you. After all the shit we've accumulated in our lives, the unhappy marriages, the misery you and I have gone through, your tragedy, we found each other and it's a beautiful thing. I thought it was a beautiful thing. In the middle of our lives. But this goddamn outrageous drinking, it's a death wish. I saw the photograph, it's a goddamn miracle you were able to walk away from that crash, and it's a goddamn miracle that old man isn't dead. I didn't even know what "point-three-two" meant, so I asked this cop I know, just to put it in some perspective, and he said he'd never heard of a number like that, that it was off the charts. He said he was surprised you weren't dead even before you got in the car. What in hell were you thinking?

MARY PAGE: Obviously I wasn't really thinking at all, Ray.

RAY: You already had two of these convictions hanging over you and you still chose to poison yourself and get behind the wheel. How am I supposed to take that? What would you have me do? Look where we are. Look where we are! You have torn our lives apart with this goddamned drinking!

MARY PAGE: Are you saying you want out of this marriage?

RAY: You're going to a penitentiary. Your daughter is barely speaking to you, I'm, I'm . . . I'm going to what, sit here, and wait for you for two goddamn years, and explain to everyone at work that my wife can't join me tonight because she's in a state prison? What am I supposed to say to my clients, when they ask me about my wife, because they all ask.

MARY PAGE: Is that what you're worried about, what you're going to tell people?

RAY: No, that's not what I'm worried about, but it's awkward, isn't it? I'm a salesman, and you may not care about it, but things like appearances make a difference. I am allowed to say that, aren't I, that you have made life, for all of the people who love you, very difficult! Not to mention that poor man suffering in the hospital right now.

MARY PAGE: I feel pretty bad about that, Ray. You piling on right now—

RAY: Do you?

MARY PAGE: Do I what?

RAY: Do you feel bad about it? Because I really can't tell.

MARY PAGE: You can't tell.

RAY: I can't tell that you feel bad about it.

MARY PAGE: I don't feel bad about it *for you.*

RAY: I don't think you do feel bad about it. I think you're so out of touch with the way you feel about anything—

MARY PAGE: Please don't tell me what I feel.

RAY: You are so out of touch with the way you feel about—

MARY PAGE *(Explodes)*: Don't tell me how I feel! You don't know how I feel! You don't know anything about the way I feel!

RAY: Okay, Mary Page—

MARY PAGE: Are we still screaming at each other?! Because I can scream! I've got a voice and I CAN SCREAM!

RAY: It's okay, please, just—

MARY PAGE: Don't tell me how I feel! Don't tell me how I feel!

RAY: Okay. Okay.

(Pause.)

MARY PAGE: I'm. I have a lot of. There is a lot on my mind. Right now. There is a lot. And we. We will get through this. We will get through. Or we won't. Or we will not get through. But we will. You will not speak to me that way, and we will work through these things. Together. Or not at all. But you will not speak to me that way. You will not tell me what I feel. And I will do this time. And I will pay this price. This is a price I am going to pay. And I will bear it, and I will pay this price, no matter how great, because it is what I must do. Because it is what I deserve. Because I am guilty.

SCENE 8

1973.

Mary Page Marlowe is twenty-seven.
Dan is older.
A motel room. Dayton, Ohio.
After sex.

DAN: We don't have to go back. To the office. *(Pause)* You don't have to rush off.

MARY PAGE: I do actually. My mother-in-law is watching my girl.

DAN: You're still on the clock. Officially.

MARY PAGE: It's after four. I have to take care of a couple of things before I get her.

DAN: What do you have to take care of?

MARY PAGE: I . . . Don't make me go through it.

DAN: Bitchy.

MARY PAGE: Okay.

DAN: Do you want a cigarette?

MARY PAGE: No, thanks.

DAN: When can I see you again?

MARY PAGE: Tomorrow morning, nine A.M. I'll be there. A little early probably.

DAN: I mean, outside of work.

MARY PAGE: I don't know. I don't want to make this some regular thing.

DAN: What's the matter with a regular thing?

MARY PAGE: I just don't have the energy for that.

DAN: Seems to me like you have a lot of energy.

MARY PAGE: Mm.

DAN: You seem very energetic.

(No response.)

I want to see you again.

MARY PAGE: Well. Maybe we can. I just, really . . . I'm not going to make this a habit, okay?

DAN: Make *me* a habit.

MARY PAGE: I, yeah.

DAN: I don't understand you.

MARY PAGE: What.

DAN: You came on so strong at the office.

MARY PAGE: I didn't come on that strong.

DAN: Pretty strong.

MARY PAGE: It wasn't that strong. You were just . . . you were on the scent.

DAN: The point is you came on to me.

MARY PAGE: Why is that the point? The point of what?

DAN: I didn't hit on you.

MARY PAGE: Maybe not.

DAN: You hit on me.

MARY PAGE: Maybe. So?

DAN: So . . . I want to see you again. And I think you should . . . I think you should see me again.

MARY PAGE: I didn't say no. I just said I can't make this a regular thing.

DAN: I think seeing me again is the right thing to do.

MARY PAGE: I don't get it, am I under some obligation to see you again?

DAN: Don't say obligation. But you hit on me.

MARY PAGE: Okay, but, so that means, what. Do I owe you something?

DAN: Don't say it like that.

MARY PAGE: Then what are you saying?

DAN: Look, didn't I just make you come? Twice?

MARY PAGE: You didn't *make* me do anything.

DAN: This was your idea.

MARY PAGE: There is no *idea*. Dan. We slept together. We both *came*. We're on equal footing here, right? Let's not keep score.

DAN: I'm your boss.

MARY PAGE: So in the *office*, we're not so equal. All right.

DAN: Look, I wouldn't be here if it weren't for you. I should be at work—

(She kisses him.)

MARY PAGE: I think you're very sexy. I like doing this with you. I'm glad we did this.

DAN: Me too.

MARY PAGE: I'm not saying we can't do it again. You get me very turned on. You're very handsome, and very sexy. You have a great, beautiful cock.

DAN: Jesus.

MARY PAGE: So let's just wait and see how it goes, okay? I'm not saying we can't do it again.

DAN: I want to do it again right now.

MARY PAGE: Yeah?

DAN: Yeah. Jesus.

MARY PAGE: Yeah, you turned on, baby?

DAN: Yeah . . .

MARY PAGE: Hold on to that and maybe we can do this again some time.

DAN: Jesus, I'm going to fuck my wife so hard tonight.

MARY PAGE: Mm.

DAN: I'm going to be thinking of you and I'll fuck my wife so hard.

MARY PAGE: Yeah . . .

DAN: Come on, let's do it again.

MARY PAGE: I can't, baby, I have to go . . .

(She breaks. He lights a cigarette, studies her.)

DAN: How long have you been married?

MARY PAGE: Not long. A few years.

DAN: Your old man must not be getting the job done. *(Pause)* Don't you worry about getting caught?

MARY PAGE: Men get caught.

(Dan thinks, laughs.)

DAN: Why is that, do you think?

MARY PAGE: They can't stand not being known.

DAN: Yeah? *(Pause)* What do you mean by that?

MARY PAGE: You? How long have you been married?

DAN: A long time. Eleven years.

MARY PAGE: But you say it's not working out.

DAN: No. I think we'll divorce.

MARY PAGE: That's too bad.

DAN: She's too old-fashioned. I shouldn't be with someone so old-fashioned.

MARY PAGE: How is she old-fashioned? Like your mom?

DAN: She doesn't like sex. What do you think of that?

MARY PAGE: Well . . . I guess I think . . . I don't know what I think. Maybe old-fashioned isn't the right word.

DAN: I need a modern girl is all. I need to be with someone who likes sex.

MARY PAGE: We should all be with someone who likes sex. If we like sex.

DAN: How old is your kid?

MARY PAGE: She's three.

DAN: Do you want to have more?

MARY PAGE: I don't think I can have more.

DAN: Are you on the pill?

MARY PAGE: No.

DAN: You're not very careful.

MARY PAGE: I don't think I can have more.

DAN: Still, don't you think you should be careful?

MARY PAGE: I know how to take care of myself.

DAN: What's her name, your daughter?

MARY PAGE: I really don't want to talk about her. Is that okay?

DAN: Yeah, sure. *(Pause)* You're a damn sexy woman. *(Pause)* Did you know that? Damn sexy. *(Pause)* You know my old man knew yours, right? Your father, I mean.

MARY PAGE: You mentioned that.

DAN: I did?

MARY PAGE: When you interviewed me, yeah.

DAN: They worked at that air-conditioning company together. North Pole.

MARY PAGE: Right.

DAN: I used to go in there after school, they'd send me out to get boxes of chicken from the Parkmoor. They had a pop machine in there, at the North Pole, where you slid the pop bottles out on this metal track. Your old man used to put the money in and let me slide the bottles out. Ed, right?

MARY PAGE: That's right.

DAN: I don't remember much about him. Those guys were real men. Veterans. I remember my old man telling me your old man had seen heavy combat somewhere.

MARY PAGE: Okinawa.

DAN *(Whistles)*: What, your old man in the Navy?

MARY PAGE: Army.

DAN: Heavy. Those fellows had a time of it. Do you know what regiment?

MARY PAGE: No.

DAN: Did he tell you stories?

MARY PAGE: No.

DAN: He skipped out, didn't he? He still alive?

MARY PAGE: I have to go.

DAN: Okay, Christ. I'm just trying to get to know you some.

MARY PAGE: I'll see you at work, okay? I'll see you tomorrow.

DAN: Okay.

(They kiss.)

What if I told you I was falling for you?

MARY PAGE: I'd say that was really lovely.

DAN: What would you say if I said I wanted to get to know you better?

MARY PAGE: I'd say I'm afraid you're going to be disappointed.

SCENE 9

1958.
> *Mary Page Marlowe is twelve.*
> *Her mother, Roberta, is thirty-two.*
> *Her parents' house. Dayton, Ohio.*

MARY PAGE *(Singing)*:
> I hear the cottonwoods whisperin' above,
> "Tammy . . . Tammy . . .
> Tammy's in love"
> The ole hootie-owl
> Hootie-hoos to the dove,
> "Tammy . . . Tammy . . .
> Tammy's in love."
>
> Does my lover feel
> What I feel

When he comes near?
My heart beats so joyfully,
You'd think that he could hear.

Wish I knew if he knew
What I'm dreamin' of
"Tammy . . . Tammy . . . Tammy's in love."

ROBERTA: Well, Mary Page, Debbie Reynolds has got nothing to worry about. *(Pause)* Why did you choose that song?

MARY PAGE: I like it.

ROBERTA: What do you like about it?

MARY PAGE: I don't know. It's pretty.

ROBERTA: I thought you were going to sing "Que Sera, Sera."

MARY PAGE: No.

ROBERTA: You told me you were going to sing "Que Sera, Sera."

MARY PAGE: No, you asked me to sing it.

ROBERTA: And you said you would.

MARY PAGE: I don't think so.

ROBERTA: Yes you did. Why don't you sing that instead?

MARY PAGE: I like "Tammy." Didn't you like it?

ROBERTA: When are you supposed to sing this?

MARY PAGE: Tomorrow. At the assembly.

ROBERTA: You got a little time. Keep practicing at it, you'll get better. I can tell you this: the way you present yourself will go a long way to cover up your voice. Stand up straight.

MARY PAGE: I am.

ROBERTA: No, you're not. Look right there, where the wall meets the ceiling. Now take a deep breath. Pull your shoulders back. Okay, now you're standing up straight.

MARY PAGE: I'm going to fall over.

ROBERTA: It's 'cause you're used to slumping.

MARY PAGE: I can't sing like this.

ROBERTA: You can't sing anyway, you might as well look good. Oh, come on now, don't get precious. Not everybody is good at everything, it's no crime.

MARY PAGE: What do you suppose I'm good at?

ROBERTA: You're so young, you got all the time in the world to find out what you're good at. You might turn out to be a great singer, you never know. People have to develop their talents.

MARY PAGE: What are you good at?

ROBERTA: Not much.

MARY PAGE: But what? Are you good at anything?

ROBERTA: I'm a pretty good card player. Hand me that ashtray. I'm a pretty good dancer. Not half bad. I have a nice figure. I can bake a cake.

MARY PAGE: You never baked me a cake.

ROBERTA: Yes I have, you just don't remember it. You got a birthday coming up, I'll make you a cake for your birthday.

MARY PAGE: You ain't gonna make me a cake.

ROBERTA: Don't say ain't. *(Pause)* Gonna be a teenager. My goodness. Do you know what you want?

MARY PAGE: I want to see *Gigi*.

ROBERTA: We can go to the pictures. But do you want anything? Want any toys or anything?

MARY PAGE: I'm too old for toys.

ROBERTA: Naw, you're just old enough to think you're too old for toys.

MARY PAGE: I don't know, some records maybe.

ROBERTA: Make me a drink, hon. We got a lot of records. What records do you want?

MARY PAGE: Ricky Nelson.

ROBERTA: Lord. We can get up that morning and go to the pictures if you want. I'll take you to the Short Stop for hamburgers, okay?

MARY PAGE: Okay.

ROBERTA: Okay. That'll be fun. And then we'll go see Grandma after, okay?

MARY PAGE: Why?

ROBERTA: 'Cause she's your grandma and she wants to see you on your birthday.

(Silence. Mary Page gives Roberta her drink.)

Where's the maraschino cherry?

MARY PAGE: You're out.

ROBERTA: Have you been eating the maraschino cherries again?

MARY PAGE: No, ma'am.

ROBERTA: Mary Page Marlowe.

MARY PAGE: I had one.

ROBERTA: You had more than one, I just bought that jar last week.

MARY PAGE: You've had a lot of old fashioneds.

ROBERTA: Listen. Sit down here, I've got to talk to you. I need you to stay with Grandma a little while.

MARY PAGE: Why?

ROBERTA: I've got to go for a little while. I'm taking a train out to California.

MARY PAGE: What for?

ROBERTA: I'm going out to see your father.

MARY PAGE: Why can't I go?

ROBERTA: 'Cause I need to go by myself.

MARY PAGE: Why?

ROBERTA: 'Cause I can't have you with me.

MARY PAGE: Why?

ROBERTA: I'm not going for long. I'm just going out to see him about some money. I don't want to take you out of school.

MARY PAGE: But I want to go.

ROBERTA: No, you need to stay here.

MARY PAGE: I don't want to stay at Grandma's.

ROBERTA: What's the matter with Grandma's?

MARY PAGE: I don't know.

ROBERTA: You love your grandma, don't you?

MARY PAGE: Yes.

ROBERTA: Then why don't you want to stay with her?

MARY PAGE: She makes me go to Mass.

ROBERTA: It's a good thing, going to church.

MARY PAGE: She makes me go a lot. She makes me go on Wednesday. That's when *Ozzie and Harriet* and *Donna Reed* are on.

ROBERTA: You are some kind of big baby. You think I care if you miss TV programs? You need to stay here.

MARY PAGE: I want to see Daddy.

ROBERTA: Mary Page. Don't fight with me now. I can't afford to take you out there with me. I need to see your father about some money and then I'm coming right back.

MARY PAGE: How long will you be gone?

ROBERTA: Two weeks. I don't know. Three weeks. I'll be back soon. You can stay in school and stay with your grandma and before you know it, I'll be back. And before I go we'll have a good birthday party, just us. Okay? *(Pause)* Okay?

MARY PAGE: Okay, Mom.

ROBERTA: Ohhh, sweetheart, you're so sensitive. *(Kisses her)* You're gonna have to toughen up some, Mary Page. The world is a mean old place. *(Kisses her again)* You practice your song now. I need to take a bath. Dick and Vicki are coming over tonight to play Yahtzee.

(Roberta exits. Mary Page sits.
Silence.)

SCENE 10

1990.

> *Mary Page Marlowe is forty-four.*
> *Her apartment. Lexington, Kentucky.*
> *Mary Page sits. Silence.*
> *She looks in an address book, dials the phone.*

MARY PAGE: Hi, Jackie, this is Mary Page Marlowe, how are you? *(Pause)* That's good. Listen, I've lost my boy. *(Pause)* Well, it's kind of a long story, he— *(Pause)* No, that's right, he did, he moved back to Dayton to live with his father. But that hasn't worked out, they haven't been getting along and now Louis has gone missing. *(Pause)* I thought . . . I know he really liked Renee, I know they were close, and I thought . . . I don't know, maybe he had hitchhiked back here to see Renee, or got the money together for a bus ticket, or— *(Pause)* You haven't? *(Pause)* Okay. Okay, well. I'm sorry to bother you with this, Jackie, he's just got me so worried, and you know how they are, he's sixteen years old— *(Pause)* Thank you. I will. *(Pause)* Okay, Jackie, thank you so much. Uh-huh. Bye-bye.

(She hangs up. She makes a drink, talks to herself:)

. . . Goddamn it . . . don't be a shit, Louis, just tell me you're okay . . . don't make me this way . . .

(Door closes, off.)

WENDY *(From off)*: Mom?

(Wendy, twenty, enters, carrying a backpack.)

MARY PAGE: I'm so glad you're here.

WENDY: What's going on?

MARY PAGE: I've gotten myself into a state. I can't shake some morbid thoughts, and I . . . I'm really glad you're here.

WENDY: So nobody has heard anything.

MARY PAGE: No, we might have tracked him down. Your father heard maybe Louis has been staying with this boy *Matt*. So your father is headed over to Matt's house to see if he's there.

WENDY: He can't just call Matt's parents?

MARY PAGE: I guess Matt has his own place or something.

WENDY: He's got his own place? A sixteen year old?

MARY PAGE: I don't know, Wendy! I don't know how old he is, what's going on, I'm not there!

WENDY: Okay, it's okay.

MARY PAGE: I'm sorry, I, I don't know. I don't really understand what's been going on up there. Louis and I haven't been talking, you know, he's so goddamn tough, and uncommunicative, and—

WENDY: It's okay, Mom.

MARY PAGE: I'm sorry. I just, I need a drink.

(Mary Page makes herself another drink.)

WENDY: So how did this start, he and Daddy got into some—

MARY PAGE: They got in a fight, and I guess it was pretty bad, Louis hit him, hit Sonny in the face—

WENDY: —Oh God—

MARY PAGE: —and then Louis screamed some ultimatums and ran out. Then Sonny eventually got him—

WENDY: Did Daddy hit *him*?

MARY PAGE: No, Sonny would never hit him, not even in self-defense, he couldn't do that.

WENDY: What started the fight?

MARY PAGE: Your father found track marks on Louis's arm and flipped out. Louis has fallen in with a bad crowd up there and . . . Louis is *struggling*. He's always *struggled*. It's just always been a hard row for him, I don't know why, he—

WENDY: So Daddy hasn't seen him since they had the fight?

MARY PAGE: No, so, Sonny got out in the truck and drove around and finally found Louis in front of the 7-Eleven, of *course*—I mean, c'mon, Louis, if you're going to be a little junkie at least try to do it a little more creatively, something with a little more originality than the fucking 7-Eleven. He said Louis was a lot calmer, he thought Louis had probably gotten high—

WENDY: Are you sure they were track marks?

MARY PAGE: What?

WENDY: Would Daddy know track marks if he saw them? 'Cause I wouldn't.

MARY PAGE: Sure you would.

WENDY: I just know them from movies.

MARY PAGE: Well, the movies make them look like real life. You would know them. I mean, would it surprise you? Forget all the pot, I caught him with coke, pills, I caught him with a sheet of acid, for heaven's sake, I didn't even think people dropped acid anymore, and he had this beautiful sheet, he's probably dealing. And you know he's on medication for his ADD and I don't know that it's helped at all, I just think it's made things worse.

WENDY: Finish your story, you said Daddy drove around and found him.

MARY PAGE: Your father found him, and said he was a lot calmer, and they had a talk. I shouldn't call it a *talk*, I don't think your little brother knows how to talk anymore, but anyway, they talked. And they agreed that it wasn't working out, living together. Your father asked him if he wanted to come back here and live with me, but Louis told him no, he hated Kentucky, and it's no secret we weren't getting on like a house on fire. You know we haven't talked in over a month, me and Louis. He won't even get on the phone and speak to me. I went up to Dayton a couple of weeks ago and tried to see him but he hid or ran away every time I came around.

WENDY: So where does he want to live?

MARY PAGE: He told Sonny that he wanted to go live with his friend, Kenny Lafferty. You remember Kenny Lafferty, the little boy that—

WENDY: I remember Kenny, the one who ate all our food.

MARY PAGE: Right, who ate all our food, all the time. So Louis said that Kenny's mother had told Louis he was welcome to stay with them until . . . whenever, she said he was welcome to stay. And your dad felt all right about that, 'cause we *know* the Laffertys, they're okay, they were always good to Louis, so okay, they had a . . . your father and Louis, they had a plan. So Sonny dropped Louis over at the Laf-